THE 2ND GRADE SPELLING WORKBOOK

95+ GAMES AND PUZZLES TO IMPROVE SPELLING SKILLS

Ann Richmond Fisher

Illustrations by Joel and Ashley Selby

ROCKRIDGE
PRESS

For general information on our other products and services or to obtain technical support, please contact our Customer Care Department within the United States at (866) 744-2665, or outside the United States at (510) 253-0500.

Rockridge Press publishes its books in a variety of electronic and print formats. Some content that appears in print may not be available in electronic books, and vice versa.

TRADEMARKS: Rockridge Press and the Rockridge Press logo are trademarks or registered trademarks of Callisto Media Inc. and/or its affiliates, in the United States and other countries, and may not be used without written permission. All other trademarks are the property of their respective owners. Rockridge Press is not associated with any product or vendor mentioned in this book.

Some of the exercises in this book previously appeared in *Word Detective*.

Series Cover Designer: Patricia Fabricant
Series Interior Designer: Brian Lewis
Art Producer: Samantha Ulban
Editor: Julie Haverkate
Production Editor: Ruth Sakata Corley
Production Manager: Martin Worthington

Illustrations © 2019 Joel and Ashley Selby

Paperback ISBN: 978-1-63878-784-6
R0

CONTENTS

INTRODUCTION

I love WORDS! That's why it's been so much fun to write this book. During my time as a classroom teacher, I wrote word games to add variety to spelling and English lessons. Word puzzles are wonderful tools for teaching spelling skills and enhancing students' vocabularies.

I would like your second grader to love words, too. I've compiled a targeted list of 180 second-grade spelling words and plugged them into more than 95 engaging games and puzzles. The words are arranged by theme, including family, friends, and animals. Students are likely to encounter most of these words in their world.

Your second grader will practice these 180 words by working through this book and completing lots of fun puzzles. Please be sure they understand the directions for each puzzle before beginning to solve it. Having difficulty with a particular word? Tell them to go on to the next word or even the next activity. You can give special attention to the words your second grader finds more difficult by keeping a word bank, a list of words your student knows, and another list of "getting there" words. This helps children focus on the possibilities and develop an "I can" mindset.

Some children will benefit from taking breaks after 20 minutes. Remind your student that no one is born knowing how to spell, read, or write. Some of my favorite words were the hardest for me to learn.

Your student is about to set off on a spelling adventure! Now turn the page to start solving these puzzles!

Words to Learn: FAMILY WORDS

Write each word in the blank.

1. mother _____

2. father _____

3. sister _____

4. brother _____

5. baby _____

6. uncle _____

7. aunt _____

8. pets _____

9. home _____

10. family _____

Write your hardest words again here:

_____

_____

_____

Merry-Go-Round

Start at any letter and move around the circle, either forward or backward, to find one of your spelling words. Circle the first letter. Write the word under each circle.

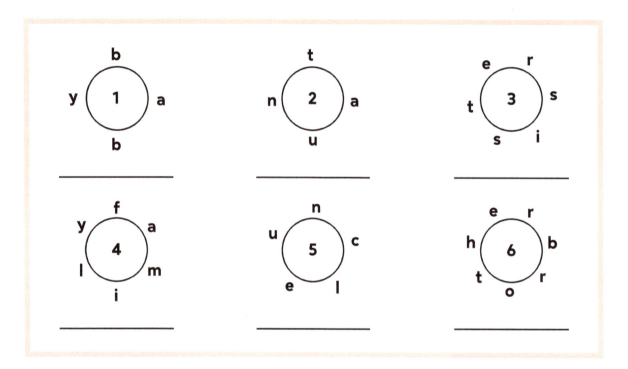

Letter Slides

Slide letters from the first word down to the second using the arrows. Keep going, sliding letters from each word down to the word below it, until you have reached the end of each slide.

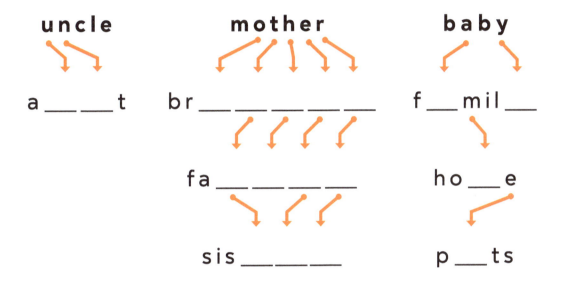

Write a sentence using one of these words.

_____

_____

Box Stop

Write one word from the box in each blank. You will not use all the words.

aunt	home	family	baby	pets
father	sister	brother	mother	uncle

1. My dad is also called my _____.

2. My mom is also called my _____.

3. My mother's brother is my _____.

4. My uncle's wife is my _____.

5. A girl who has the same parents as I do is my _____.

6. A boy who has the same parents as I do is my _____.

7. The place where I live is my _____.

8. My animals are my _____.

Places, Please

Add each of your spelling words to this puzzle. Use the letters shown to help you. Write your word again in the blank.

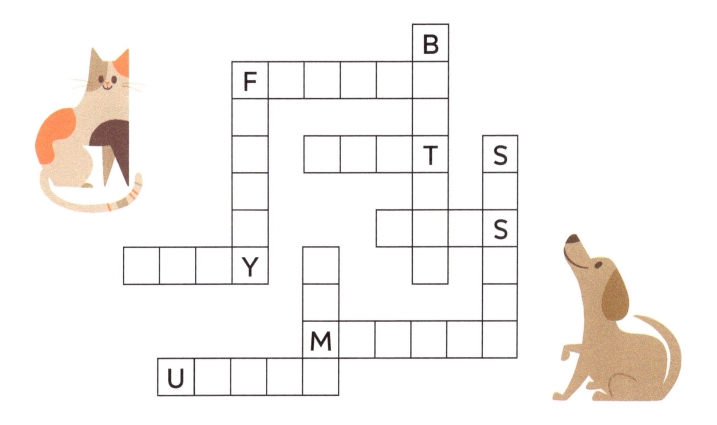

uncle _____   baby _____

aunt _____   sister _____

pets _____   brother _____

home _____   mother _____

family _____   father _____

Be Choosy!

Choose the best answer and circle it. Write the word in the blank.

1. Sometimes I visit my aunt and _____.

   home   pets   uncle

2. When my _____ brother was born, I helped take

   care of him.

   sister   baby   father

3. Because my _____ is a pilot, he does not come

   home every night.

   father   mother   sister

4. After school, I give my _____ fresh food and water.

   family   pets   home

5. I asked my _____ if she would play ball with me.

   sister   baby   brother

Words to Learn: MORE FAMILY WORDS

Write each word in the blank.

1. child   _____

2. parent   _____

3. grandpa   _____

4. grandma   _____

5. love   _____

6. trust   _____

7. sharing   _____

8. caring   _____

9. helpful   _____

10. together   _____

Write your hardest words again here:

_____

_____

_____

Tic-Tac-Toe

Circle every word that is spelled correctly. Draw a line through three correct words to score a tic-tac-toe. Write the misspelled words correctly on the lines below.

granpa	careing	parent
togther	helpful	love
grandma	trust	shareing

_____

_____

_____

Word Search

Circle each word you find in the word search. Words may go up, down, or across, both backward and forward. Write each word as you find it.

L	G	U	A	R	D	L	I	H	C
O	G	R	A	N	D	M	A	R	E
V	J	P	G	P	J	S	T	K	F
E	J	A	R	M	H	H	O	E	G
U	C	R	A	Z	E	A	G	X	T
B	A	E	N	Y	L	R	E	Z	R
Q	R	N	D	C	P	I	T	E	U
K	I	T	P	E	F	N	H	C	S
H	N	U	A	Z	U	G	E	Z	T
L	G	Z	H	Q	L	N	R	L	A

grandpa _____   together _____

grandma _____   caring _____

parent _____   sharing _____

child _____   love _____

helpful _____   trust _____

Be Choosy!

Choose the best answer and circle it. Write the word in the blank.

1. It's fun to work _____ as a family.

   trust   love   together

2. My father is a _____.

   parent   helpful   grandma

3. Your mother's mother is your _____.

   grandpa   grandma   child

4. I _____ to spend time with family.

   trust   love   caring

5. My sister and I like _____ treats from our grandma.

   caring   sharing   trust

Crack the Code

Use the code provided to find your spelling words. Write each letter as you solve it.

1. 6 8 ! # 6

    __ __ __ __ __

2. # 4 2 8 ^ 3 7

    __ __ __ __ __ __ __

3. 9 1 + 5

    __ __ __ __

4. 7 8 2 3 ? & 2

    __ __ __ __ __ __ __

5. & 2 8 5 3 6

    __ __ __ __ __ __

6. 7 8 2 3 ? * 2

    __ __ __ __ __ __ __

1 = o	2 = a	3 = n
4 = h	5 = e	6 = t
7 = g	8 = r	9 = l
* = m	+ = v	? = d
! = u	# = s	^ = i
& = p		

Missing Letters

Add the missing letters to finish the spelling words.

1. h __ __ e

2. t r __ __ __

3. __ h a __ i __ g

4. c __ i __ __

5. p a __ __ __ t

6. c a __ __ __ g

7. h e __ __ __ u __

8. t __ __ e t __ __ r

Write a sentence using one of these words.

_____

_____

Words to Learn: FRIENDSHIP WORDS

Write each word in the blank.

1. pal _____

2. buddy _____

3. grin _____

4. funny _____

5. group _____

6. team _____

7. games _____

8. toys _____

9. inside _____

10. outside _____

Write your hardest words again here:

_____

_____

_____

Scrambles

Write the correct spelling word for each set of scrambled letters.

1. n r i g   _ _ _ _ _ _

2. u p o r g   _ _ _ _ _ _ _

3. s y o t   _ _ _ _ _ _

4. n u n y f   _ _ _ _ _ _

5. s m e a g   _ _ _ _ _ _

6. s t i o d u e   _ _ _ _ _ _ _ _ _

7. d u b y d   _ _ _ _ _ _

8. d i s e n i   _ _ _ _ _ _ _

Write a sentence using one of these words.

_____

_____

Box Stop

Write the correct words from the box in each blank. You will not use all the words.

group	inside	grin	outside	pal
games	buddy	funny	toys	team

1. What two words have almost the same meaning

   as "friend"?

   _____   _____

2. What two words can mean "more than one person"?

   _____   _____

3. What two words are opposites?

   _____   _____

4. What two things can you use when you play?

   _____   _____

PUZZLE 13

Word Search

Circle each word you find in the word search. Words may go up, down, or across, both backward and forward. Write each word as you find it.

T	F	E	D	I	S	T	U	O
H	S	Z	F	S	Y	O	T	A
L	G	I	I	N	S	I	D	E
E	R	G	U	Y	N	N	U	F
S	O	R	E	Q	L	M	V	T
P	U	I	A	J	K	N	R	E
A	P	N	W	Y	V	R	L	A
L	W	G	A	M	E	S	N	M
X	Y	Y	D	D	U	B	M	I

inside _____   grin _____

outside _____   group _____

team _____   buddy _____

games _____   pal _____

funny _____   toys _____

Tic-Tac-Toe

Circle every word that is spelled correctly. Draw a line through three correct words to score a tic-tac-toe. Write the misspelled words correctly on the lines below.

buddie	gruop	games
team	grin	inside
toyes	funy	otside

_____

_____

_____

Places, Please

Add each of your spelling words to this puzzle. Use the letters shown to help you. Write your word again in the blank.

funny _____   games _____

grin _____   inside _____

group _____   outside _____

team _____   pal _____

toys _____   buddy _____

Words to Learn: MORE FRIENDSHIP WORDS

Write each word in the blank.

1. children   _____

2. birthday   _____

3. party   _____

4. balloon   _____

5. talk   _____

6. laugh   _____

7. listen   _____

8. joke   _____

9. give   _____

10. friend   _____

Write your hardest words again here:

_____

_____

_____

Match Up

When we write, some letters reach above the line and some go below it. Look at the shapes to help you find the right spelling word and write it in the matching shape.

joke	give	talk	laugh	listen	party

1.
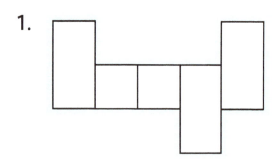

2.
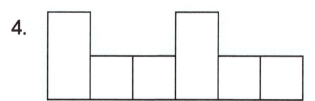

3.
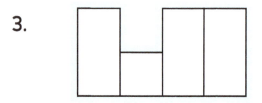

4.

5.
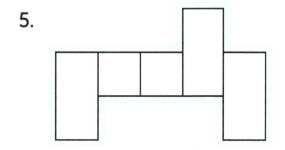

6.
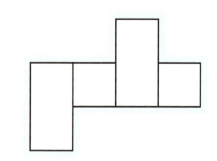

Scrambles

Write the correct spelling word for each set of scrambled letters.

1. k a t l   __ __ __ __

2. o k j e   __ __ __ __

3. e d i f r n   __ __ __ __ __ __

4. t a y r p   __ __ __ __ __

5. h u g a l   __ __ __ __ __

6. s i l n e t   __ __ __ __ __ __

7. l d e h i n c r __ __ __ __ __ __ __ __ __

8. o n l a o b l __ __ __ __ __ __ __

Write a sentence using one of these words.

_____

_____

Be Choosy!

Choose the best answer and circle it. Write the word in the blank.

1. On my next _____, I will be seven years old.

   joke   friend   birthday

2. I can hear lots of _____ playing in the park.

   listen   children   friend

3. It's fun to tell a good _____.

   joke   laugh   party

4. I will _____ my friend a gift at his party.

   laugh   give   joke

5. When I let go of the _____, it floated in the air.

   friend   balloon   party

Merry-Go-Round

Start at any letter and move around the circle, either forward or backward, to find one of your spelling words. Circle the first letter. Write the word under each circle.

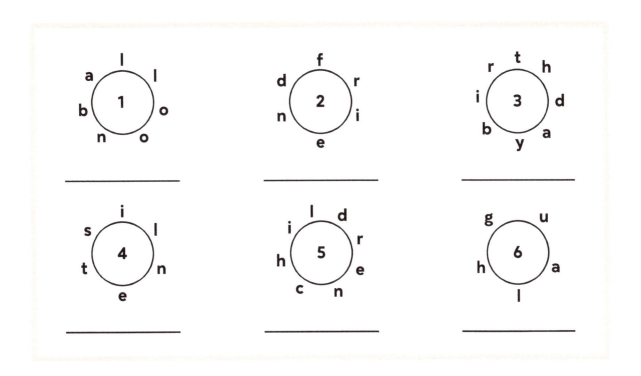

Box Stop

Write the correct word from the box in each blank. You will not use all the words.

party	listen	give	birthday	balloon
laugh	children	friend	talk	joke

1. I like to play with my best _____.

2. I always _____ when I hear a

   funny _____.

3. Can you please _____ to what I am saying?

4. I will plan a _____ for my

   pal's _____.

5. I will _____ to you on the phone soon.

Words to Learn: SCHOOL WORDS

Write each word in the blank.

1. add _____

2. count _____

3. write _____

4. spell _____

5. read _____

6. draw _____

7. paint _____

8. think _____

9. work _____

10. learn _____

Write your hardest words again here:

_____

_____

_____

Match Up

When we write, some letters reach above the line and some go below it. Look at the shapes to help you find the right spelling word and write it in the matching shape.

| count | paint | think | learn | write | spell |

1.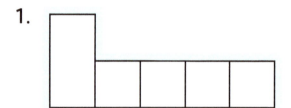

2.

3.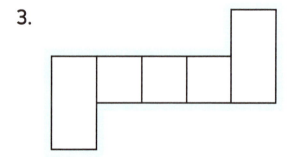

4.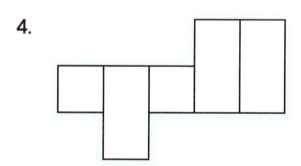

5.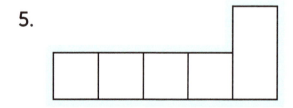

6.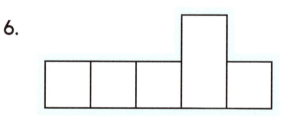

Letter Slides

Slide letters from the first word down to the second using the arrows. Keep going, sliding letters from each word down to the word below it, until you have reached the end of each slide.

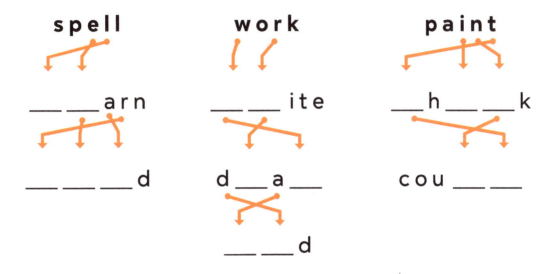

Write a sentence using one of these words.

_____

_____

Tic-Tac-Toe

Circle every word that is spelled correctly. Draw a line through three correct words to score a tic-tac-toe. Write the misspelled words correctly on the lines below.

read	cont	drau
spel	add	werk
lern	write	paint

_____

_____

_____

1 2 3

Be Choosy!

Choose the best answer and circle it. Write the word in the blank.

1. My sister and I like to _____ books together.

   add   think   read

2. I want to _____ new spelling words.

   count   learn   work

3. My little brother can _____ to 10.

   paint   write   count

4. I can _____ 10 plus 20.

   add   think   spell

5. If we _____ hard now, we can play games later.

   paint   work   draw

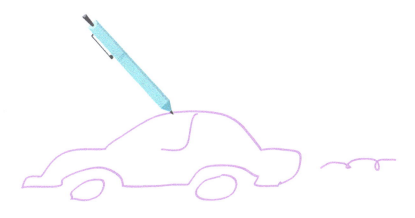

Places, Please

Add each of your spelling words to this puzzle. Use the letters shown to help you. Write your word again in the blank.

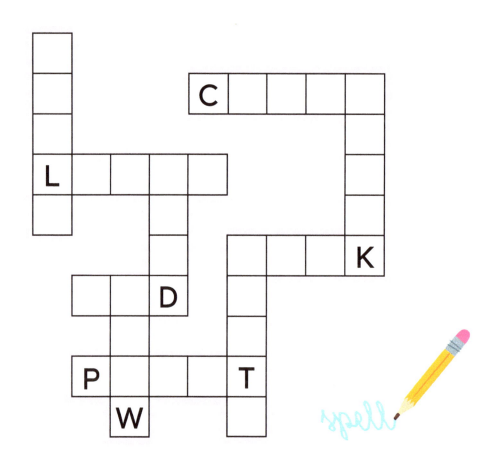

learn _____   spell _____

work _____   write _____

paint _____   count _____

draw _____   add _____

read _____   think _____

Words to Learn: MORE SCHOOL WORDS

Write each word in the blank.

1. paper   _____
2. pencil   _____
3. desk   _____
4. shelf   _____
5. class   _____
6. teacher   _____
7. grade   _____
8. study   _____
9. backpack   _____
10. lunchroom   _____

Write your hardest words again here:

_____

_____

_____

Missing Letters

Add the missing letters to finish the spelling words.

1. p __ n __ __ l

2. t __ __ __ __ e r

3. s __ __ __ f

4. s __ __ d __

5. __ a __ e __

6. __ e __ __

7. b __ __ __ p __ __ __

8. l __ n __ __ r __ __ m

Write a sentence using one of these words.

_____

_____

Merry-Go-Round

Start at any letter and move around the circle, either forward or backward, to find one of your spelling words. Circle the first letter. Write the word under each circle.

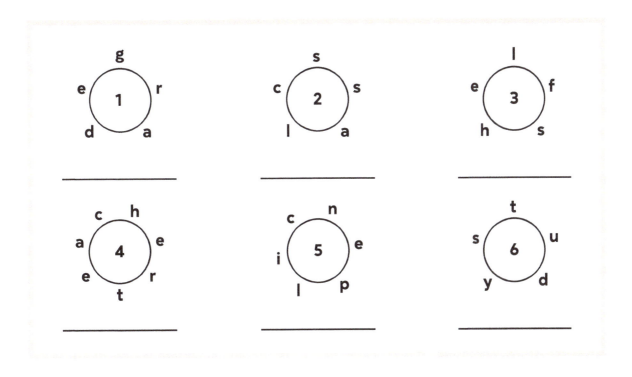

Box Stop

Write the correct word from the box in each blank. You will not use all the words.

shelf	teacher	pencil	backpack	paper
study	class	grade	desk	lunchroom

1. What word describes all the students in your room?

    _____

2. What three words tell where you can put your books?

    _____   _____   _____

3. Who helps you learn new things? _____

4. What word tells the place where you can eat?

    _____

5. What word tells what you do to learn facts?_____

6. What can you sharpen? _____

Word Search

Circle each word you find in the word search. Words may go up, down, or across, both backward and forward. Write each word as you find it.

S	Q	Z	L	I	C	N	E	P
H	S	S	B	K	J	V	Z	J
E	T	Y	A	E	D	A	R	G
L	U	N	C	H	R	O	O	M
F	D	W	K	W	V	A	L	C
N	Y	D	P	G	Z	A	W	L
A	I	P	A	P	E	R	J	A
R	E	H	C	A	E	T	Q	S
P	Y	E	K	S	E	D	G	S

lunchroom _____   desk _____

backpack _____   study _____

class _____   pencil _____

grade _____   paper _____

teacher _____   shelf _____

Scrambles

Write the correct spelling word for each set of scrambled letters.

1. c l i p n e _____

2. e h l f s _____

3. d a g e r _____

4. s k e d _____

5. c r a t e h e _____

6. a p p r e _____

7. a a b c c k k p _____

8. s c l a s _____

Write a sentence using one of these words.

_____

_____

Write each word in the blank.

1. dog _____

2. fish _____

3. frog _____

4. duck _____

5. chicken _____

6. kitten _____

7. rabbit _____

8. sheep _____

9. goat _____

10. horse _____

Write your hardest words again here:

_____

_____

_____

Letter Slides

Slide letters from the first word down to the second using the arrows. Keep going, sliding letters from each word down to the word below it, until you have reached the end of each slide.

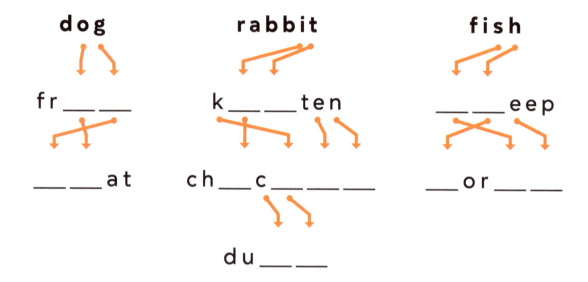

Write a sentence using one of these words.

_____

_____

Match Up

When we write, some letters reach above the line and some go below it. Look at the shapes to help you find the right spelling word and write it in the matching shape.

| frog | horse | rabbit | kitten | duck | sheep |

1.

2.

3.

4.

5.

6.

Be Choosy!

Choose the best answer and circle it. Write the word in the blank.

1. This _____ lays an egg every day.

    chicken   fish   kitten

2. A puppy grows up to be a _____.

    frog   rabbit   dog

3. A lamb grows up to be a _____.

    horse   sheep   duck

4. A _____ grows up to be a cat.

    dog   kitten   goat

5. A _____ says, "Quack!"

    goat   duck   rabbit

Tic-Tac-Toe

Circle every word that is spelled correctly. Draw a line through three correct words to score a tic-tac-toe. Write the misspelled words correctly on the lines below.

kiten	chiken	sheep
rabit	frog	gote
duck	fish	shepe

_____

_____

_____

Follow the Clues

Write the spelling words that fit each clue. There will be several answers at first. You will write some spelling words more than once. For the last clue, there will be just one word. Which word will it be?

dog	fish	frog	duck	chicken
kitten	rabbit	sheep	goat	horse

1. Six animals with four legs

    _____   _____   _____

    _____   _____   _____

2. Two animals with four legs that are spelled with six letters

    _____   _____

3. One animal with four legs, spelled with six letters, and

    that has a short, furry tail _____

Words to Learn: MORE ANIMAL WORDS

Write each word in the blank.

1. whale   _____

2. snail   _____

3. shark   _____

4. lion   _____

5. tiger   _____

6. camel   _____

7. snake   _____

8. goose   _____

9. ladybug   _____

10. butterfly   _____

Write your hardest words again here:

_____

_____

_____

Scrambles

Write the correct spelling word for each set of scrambled letters.

1. m e c a l   _ _ _ _ _
2. g r i t e   _ _ _ _ _
3. o s e o g   _ _ _ _ _
4. k e n a s   _ _ _ _ _
5. g l y a b u d   _ _ _ _ _ _ _
6. l a w e h   _ _ _ _ _
7. r h a s k   _ _ _ _ _
8. t r u f b y e l t   _ _ _ _ _ _ _ _ _

Write a sentence using one of these words.

Box Stop

Write the correct word from the box in each blank. You will not use all the words.

> whale   shark   snail   tiger   lion
>
> camel   snake   goose   ladybug   butterfly

1. Which two words rhyme?

    _____   _____

2. Which two words share three of the same letters in the same order?

    _____   _____

3. Which three animals can fly?

    _____   _____   _____

4. Which two animals always live in the water?

    _____   _____

5. Which animal would you most like to ride?

    _____

Match Up

When we write, some letters reach above the line and some go below it. Look at the shapes to help you find the right spelling word and write it in the matching shape.

| camel | tiger | lion | goose | snake | whale |

1.

2.

3.

4.

5.

6.

Word Search

Circle each word you find in the word search. Words may go up, down, or across, both backward and forward. Write each word as you find it.

L	C	E	L	E	N	O	I	L
I	G	L	E	S	H	A	R	K
A	E	A	M	O	V	K	Y	D
N	E	H	A	O	E	V	G	B
S	L	W	C	G	T	H	P	V
Y	L	F	R	E	T	T	U	B
T	I	G	E	R	H	U	T	R
U	C	L	A	D	Y	B	U	G
J	P	Q	G	E	K	A	N	S

lion _____   snail _____

tiger _____   shark _____

camel _____   whale _____

goose _____   ladybug _____

snake _____   butterfly _____

Crack the Code

Use the code to find your spelling words. Write each letter as you
solve it.

1. Ω 6 ¶ 5 7

    — — — — —

2. ➜ ¥ ¥ Ω 3

    — — — — —

3. 1 ✳ ¶ 7 3

    — — — — —

4. Ω 6 ¶ 4 3

    — — — — —

5. 2 5 ➜ 3 @

    — — — — —

6. Ω ✳ ¶ @ 4

    — — — — —

1 = w	2 = t	3 = e
4 = k	5 = i	6 = n
7 = l	@ = r	¶ = a
➜ = g	¥ = o	Ω = s
✳ = h		

Words to Learn: OUTDOOR WORDS

Write each word in the blank.

1. grass _____

2. trees _____

3. water _____

4. pond _____

5. pool _____

6. air _____

7. walk _____

8. skip _____

9. jump _____

10. climb _____

Write your hardest words again here:

_____

_____

_____

Letter Slides

Slide letters from the first word down to the second using the arrows. Keep going, sliding letters from each word down to the word below it, until you have reached the end of each slide.

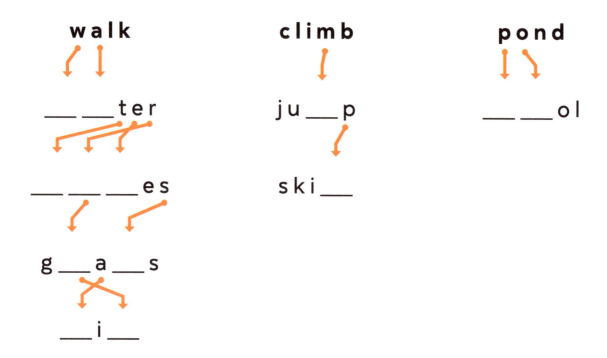

walk

___ ___ t e r

___ ___ ___ e s

g ___ a ___ s

___ i ___

climb

j u ___ p

s k i ___

pond

___ ___ o l

Write a sentence using one of these words.

_____

_____

Be Choosy!

Choose the best answer and circle it. Write the word in the blank.

1. We need to drink _____ every day.

   water   grass   air

2. How high can you _____ in a tree?

   walk   path   climb

3. I like to swim in the indoor _____ .

   pond   pool   grass

4. It's fun to go on a _____ with a friend.

   walk   jump   air

5. It was hard for me to learn to _____ .

   trees   skip   pool

Box Stop

Write the correct word from the box in each blank. You will not use all the words.

walk	trees	water	pond	jump
air	grass	skip	pool	climb

1. What four words tell what you can do at the park?

    _____   _____

    _____   _____

2. Which word describes the thing you most like to do?

    _____

3. What two words name things that hold water?

    _____   _____

4. What two things grow?

    _____   _____

5. Write a sentence that uses two words from the box.

    _____

    _____

Scrambles

Write the correct spelling word for each set of scrambled letters.

1. k a l w   __ __ __ __

2. s a g s r   __ __ __ __ __ __

3. m u p j   __ __ __ __ __

4. t r a w e   __ __ __ __ __ __

5. l o p o   __ __ __ __

6. n o d p   __ __ __ __

7. b l i m c   __ __ __ __ __

8. k s p i   __ __ __ __

Write a sentence using one of these words.

Letter Sense

Add the missing letters to your spelling words so each sentence makes sense.

1. The warm summer ___ ___ r feels nice.

2. We have shade from the tall t ___ ___ ___ s.

3. Do you like to play ___ ___ ___ p rope?

4. Dad can catch fish in our ___ ___ n ___ .

5. It is time to mow our g ___ ___ ___ ___ again.

6. W ___ ___ ___ ___ is good for many things.

Words to Learn: MORE OUTDOOR WORDS

Write each word in the blank.

1. birds _____

2. flowers _____

3. path _____

4. slide _____

5. sandbox _____

6. playground _____

7. kites _____

8. wind _____

9. camping _____

10. sunshine _____

Write your hardest words again here:

_____

_____

_____

Merry-Go-Round

Start at any letter and move around the circle, either forward or back-ward, to find one of your spelling words. Circle the first letter. Write the word under each circle.

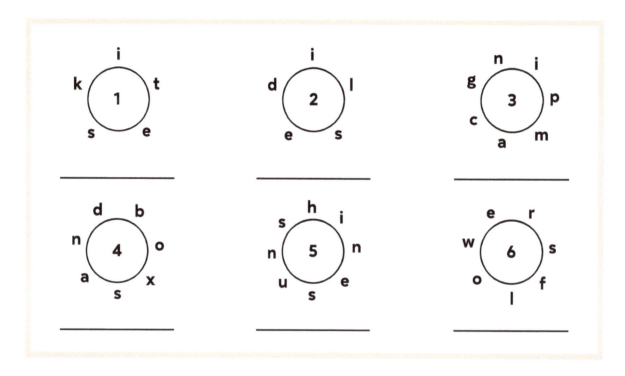

_____

_____

_____

_____

_____

_____

Word Search

Circle each word you find in the word search. Words may go up, down, across, or diagonally, both backward and forward. Write each word as you find it.

P	C	G	R	K	I	T	E	S	C	D
U	L	G	N	I	P	M	A	C	K	X
B	D	A	X	R	J	F	L	Z	O	X
B	I	M	Y	I	Q	I	B	B	G	F
F	X	R	S	G	O	B	D	Y	H	L
U	M	R	D	B	R	N	T	S	T	O
D	N	I	W	S	A	O	E	Q	A	W
Z	H	L	K	S	W	D	U	Q	P	E
S	U	N	S	H	I	N	E	N	R	R
L	R	L	Y	L	V	W	B	T	D	S
A	N	G	S	W	E	G	A	I	H	O

birds _____   playground _____

flowers _____   kites _____

path _____   wind _____

slide _____   camping _____

sandbox _____   sunshine _____

Be Choosy!

Choose the best answer and circle it. Write the word in the blank.

1. There are many things to play on

    at the _____.

    slide   sandbox   playground

2. My kite will fly well if there is some _____.

    sunshine   birds   wind

3. Let's walk along this _____.

    camping   path   sandbox

4. My little sister likes to play with toys and trucks

    in the _____.

    kites   sandbox   path

5. I enjoy smelling the lovely _____ at the park.

    flowers   wind   birds

Crack the Code

Use the code to find your spelling words. Write each letter as you solve it.

1. _ € 2 § ♠

—— —— —— —— ——

2. 3 € 1 §

—— —— —— ——

3. ♠ 7 € § o

—— —— —— —— ——

4. 4 7 6 3 o 2 ♠

—— —— —— —— —— —— ——

5. 5 € ? o ♠

—— —— —— —— ——

6. ♠ 8 1 § _ 6 ✳

—— —— —— —— —— —— ——

1 = n	2 = r	3 = w
4 = f	5 = k	6 = o
7 = l	8 = a	♠ = s
? = t	_ = b	€ = i
o = e	✳ = x	§ = d

Follow the Clues

Write the spelling words that fit each clue. There will be several answers at first. You will write some spelling words more than once. For the last clue, there will be just one word. Which word will it be?

sunshine	wind	sandbox	playground	camping
kites	flowers	birds	slide	path

1. Three words that mean there is "more than one"

   _____ _____ _____

2. Two things that fly

   _____ _____

3. One thing that flies and is not made by people

   _____

Write a sentence that uses any word from the box.

_____

_____

Words to Learn: COLORS

Write each word in the blank.

1. red _____

2. blue _____

3. green _____

4. yellow _____

5. white _____

6. black _____

7. gold _____

8. brown _____

9. orange _____

10. purple _____

Write your hardest words again here:

_____

_____

_____

Scrambles

Write the correct spelling word for each set of scrambled letters.

1. d e r   _ _ _

2. l e w o l y   _ _ _ _ _ _

3. l o g d   _ _ _ _

4. u l e b   _ _ _ _

5. l u p p r e   _ _ _ _ _ _

6. t w e i h   _ _ _ _ _

7. g r o a n e   _ _ _ _ _ _

8. k a l c b   _ _ _ _ _

Write a sentence using one of these words.

_____

_____

Box Stop

Write the correct word from the box in each blank. You will not use all the words.

brown	black	white	blue	orange
red	gold	green	purple	yellow

1. The color of treasure or jewelry _____

2. The color of the letters in this book _____

3. Two colors you might use to color the sun

    _____   _____

4. The color of snow _____

5. The color of the sky on a clear day _____

6. The color of mud _____

7. The color you get when you mix red and blue _____

Words to Learn: Colors   63

Tic-Tac-Toe

Circle every color that is spelled correctly. Draw a line through three correct words to score a tic-tac-toe. Write the misspelled words correctly in the blanks.

read	yelow	black
blew	white	perple
green	broun	gold

_____

_____

_____

Missing Letters

Add the missing letters to finish the spelling words.

1. b ___ ___ e

2. g ___ ___ ___ n

3. ___ ___ ___ d

4. b ___ ___ ___ n

5. ___ ___ a n ___ ___

6. p ___ ___ p ___ ___

7. ___ e ___ ___ o ___

8. ___ h ___ ___ e

Write a sentence using one of these words.

_____

_____

Places, Please

Add each of your spelling words to this puzzle. Use the letters shown to help you. Write your word again in the blank.

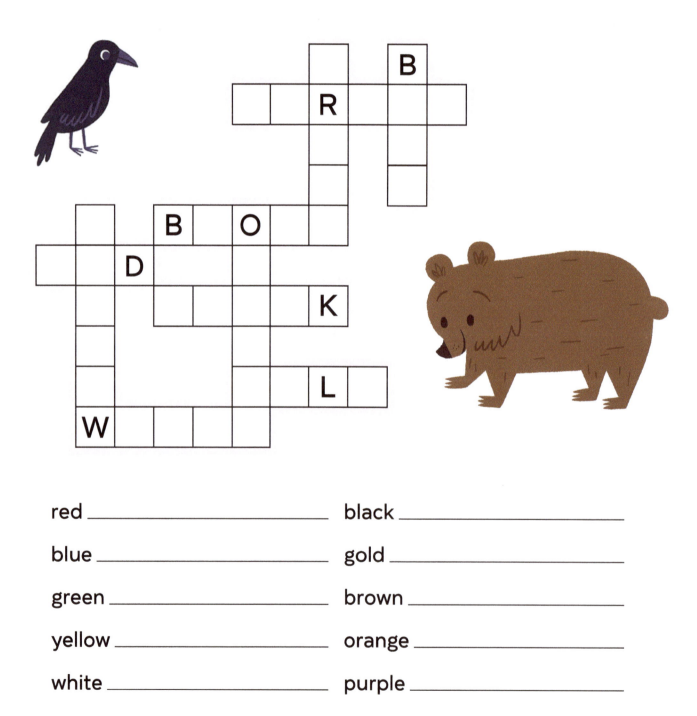

red _____   black _____

blue _____   gold _____

green _____   brown _____

yellow _____   orange _____

white _____   purple _____

Words to Learn: NUMBERS

Write each word in the blank.

1. zero   _____

2. four   _____

3. five   _____

4. six   _____

5. seven   _____

6. eight   _____

7. nine   _____

8. ten   _____

9. eleven   _____

10. twelve   _____

Write your hardest words again here:

_____

_____

_____

Be Choosy!

Choose the best answer for each number pattern and circle it. Write the word in the blank.

1. One, two, three, . . . _____

   four   five   six

2. Ten, nine, eight, . . . _____

   nine   seven   six

3. Two, four, six, . . . _____

   eight   ten   eleven

4. Eight, nine, ten, . . . _____

   twelve   eleven   seven

5. Three, two, one, . . . _____

   four   five   zero

6. One, three, five, . . . _____

   six   seven   four

Word Search

Circle each word you find in the word search. Words may go up, down, across, or diagonally, both backward and forward. Write each word as you find it.

B	V	X	P	N	E	V	E	S
O	E	F	I	E	V	X	I	S
R	S	L	W	U	I	F	W	E
E	K	T	E	D	N	G	X	S
Z	O	M	W	V	Y	I	H	O
E	F	Z	J	E	E	J	N	T
R	M	O	A	M	L	N	L	E
N	E	T	U	F	I	V	E	S
Q	N	A	R	R	L	Z	E	T

zero _____ eight _____

four _____ nine _____

five _____ ten _____

six _____ eleven _____

seven _____ twelve _____

Letter Slides

Slide letters from the first word down to the second using the arrows. Keep going, sliding letters from each word down to the word below it, until you have reached the end of each slide.

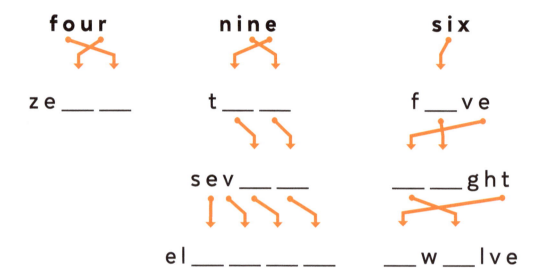

four

z e ___ ___

nine

t ___ ___

s e v ___ ___

e l ___ ___ ___ ___

six

f ___ v e

___ ___ g h t

___ w ___ l v e

Write a sentence using one of these words.

_____

_____

Follow the Clues

Write the spelling words that fit each clue. There will be several answers at first. You will write some spelling words more than once. For the last clue, there will be just one word. Which word will it be?

zero	four	five	six	seven
eight	nine	ten	eleven	twelve

1. Four odd numbers greater than four

   _____   _____   _____   _____

2. Two odd numbers greater than four, spelled with five or more letters

   _____   _____

3. One odd number greater than four, spelled with five or more letters, and written with two digits _____

Number Chart

Write the missing number words in this number chart.

0	
1	one
2	two
3	three
4	
5	
6	
7	
8	
9	
10	
11	
12	
13	thirteen
14	fourteen

Words to Learn: FEELINGS

Write each word in the blank.

1. glad _____

2. sad _____

3. happy _____

4. scared _____

5. silly _____

6. safe _____

7. mean _____

8. lost _____

9. angry _____

10. strong _____

Write your hardest words again here:

_____

_____

_____

Merry-Go-Round

Start at any letter and move around the circle, either forward or backward, to find one of your spelling words. Circle the first letter. Write the word under each circle.

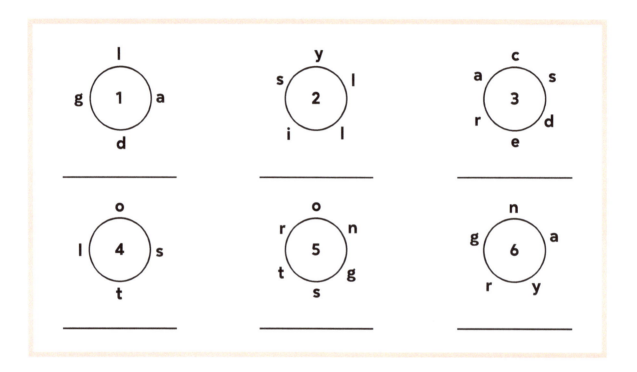

Box Stop

Write the correct word from the box in each blank. You will not use all the words.

glad	angry	happy	scared	silly
safe	lost	mean	sad	strong

1. What two words rhyme?

    _____   _____

2. What word has almost the same meaning as

    "happy"? _____

3. What word has the same meaning as "mad"? _____

4. What word can have the same meaning as "funny"?

    _____

5. What word tells how you might feel if you were alone

    during a storm? _____

6. Write a sentence about a time when you felt strong.

Match Up

When we write, some letters reach above the line and some go below it. Look at the shapes to help you find the right spelling word and write it in the matching shape.

| lost | strong | angry | safe | scared | silly |

1.

2.

3.

4.

5.

6.

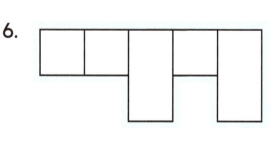

Scrambles

Write the correct spelling word for each set of scrambled letters.

1. p a p h y   _ _ _ _ _

2. s o l t   _ _ _ _

3. l a g d   _ _ _ _

4. n y a g r   _ _ _ _ _

5. i s l y l   _ _ _ _ _

6. a s d   _ _ _

7. c e r d a s   _ _ _ _ _ _

8. g r o s n t   _ _ _ _ _ _

Write a sentence using one of these words.

_____

_____

Places, Please

Add each of your spelling words to this puzzle. Use the letters shown to help you. Write your word again in the blank.

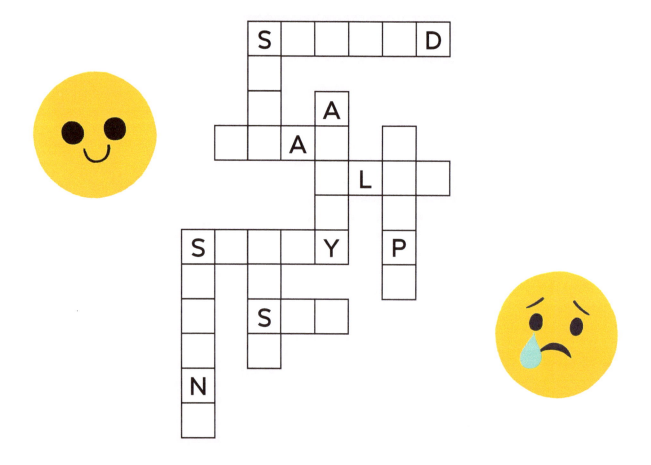

glad _____   strong _____

sad _____   lost _____

happy _____   mean _____

scared _____   angry _____

safe _____   silly _____

Words to Learn: MORE FEELINGS

Write each word in the blank.

1. sorry   _____

2. cross   _____

3. joyful   _____

4. thankful   _____

5. hurt   _____

6. proud   _____

7. bored   _____

8. gloomy   _____

9. afraid   _____

10. hopeful   _____

Write your hardest words again here:

_____

_____

_____

Letter Slides

Slide letters from the first word down to the second using the arrows. Keep going, sliding letters from each word down to the word below it, until you have reached the end of each slide.

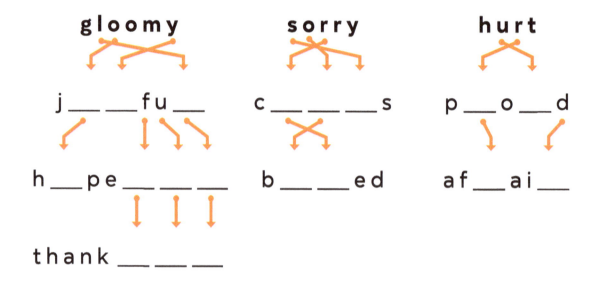

gloomy

j ___ ___ f u ___

h ___ p e ___ ___ ___

t h a n k ___ ___ ___

sorry

c ___ ___ ___ ___ s

b ___ ___ e d

hurt

p ___ o ___ d

a f ___ a i ___

Write a sentence using one of these words.

_____

_____

Be Choosy!

Choose the best answer and circle it. Write the word in the blank.

1. You did your best work and I am very _____ of you!

    proud   cross   afraid

2. I cannot find anything to do, so I am very _____.

    hurt   bored   sorry

3. We are _____ that the day will be sunny tomorrow.

    gloomy   cross   hopeful

4. My dog feels _____ when there are storms.

    joyful   afraid   thankful

5. Sometimes I get _____ when I don't feel well.

    cross   proud   joyful

6. I am very _____ for your help!

    thankful   sorry   afraid

Tic-Tac-Toe

Circle every word that is spelled correctly. Draw a line through three correct words to score a tic-tac-toe. Write the misspelled words correctly on the lines below.

bord	afriad	thankful
glomy	hert	proud
sorry	hopful	joyful

_____

_____

_____

Word Search

Circle each word you find in the word search. Words may go up, down, across, or diagonally, both backward and forward. Write each word as you find it.

Y	T	I	O	G	R	T	R	U	H
U	C	H	S	O	R	R	Y	C	S
W	E	R	A	V	M	Z	R	D	G
D	D	Q	O	N	D	I	A	E	W
D	U	T	O	S	K	H	Z	R	L
H	O	M	Z	I	S	F	Y	O	U
H	R	H	U	P	V	Y	U	B	F
L	P	H	O	P	E	F	U	L	Y
D	I	A	R	F	A	F	K	B	O
G	L	O	O	M	Y	S	P	S	J

joyful _____ cross _____

thankful _____ bored _____

hopeful _____ proud _____

gloomy _____ sorry _____

afraid _____ hurt _____

Letter Sense

Add the missing letters to your spelling words so each sentence makes sense.

1. When you are full of joy, you are ___ ___ ___ ___ ___ l.

2. I am so ___ ___ ___ ___ y that I ___ ___ r ___ your feelings!

3. It has been cloudy all week and I feel g ___ ___ ___ ___ ___.

4. What shall we do so we won't be b ___ ___ ___ ___?

5. We are ___ o ___ ___ ___ u ___ that we will go on a trip soon.

6. I am ___ ___ o ___ ___ of my little sister for learning to ride a scooter!

Words to Learn: AT HOME WORDS

Write each word in the blank.

1. house   _____

2. roof   _____

3. floor   _____

4. door   _____

5. stove   _____

6. sink   _____

7. room   _____

8. table   _____

9. chairs   _____

10. broom   _____

Write your hardest words again here:

_____

_____

_____

Box Stop

Write the correct word from the box in each blank. You will not use all the words.

house	roof	floor	broom	door
room	chairs	table	sink	stove

1. What two words rhyme with "zoom"?

   _____   _____

2. What word is like "home"?

   _____

3. What two words rhyme with "or"?

   _____   _____

4. What word names a place where you could wash?

   _____

5. What word names the top of a house? _____

6. Choose one word to use in a sentence.

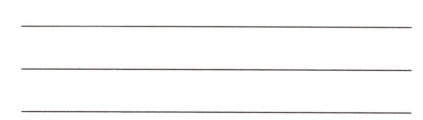

Merry-Go-Round

Start at any letter and move around the circle, either forward or backward, to find one of your spelling words. Circle the first letter. Write the word under each circle.

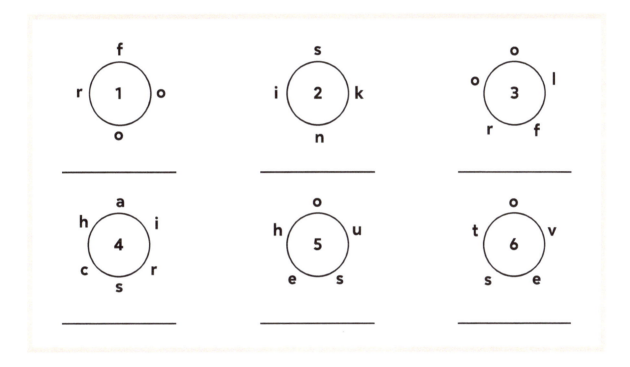

Scrambles

Write the correct spelling word for each set of scrambled letters.

1. f o r o l   __ __ __ __ __

2. o r o m b   __ __ __ __ __

3. k n i s   __ __ __ __

4. t e s v o   __ __ __ __ __

5. o o r d   __ __ __ __

6. s e u h o   __ __ __ __ __

7. s i c a h r   __ __ __ __ __ __

8. b l e a t   __ __ __ __ __

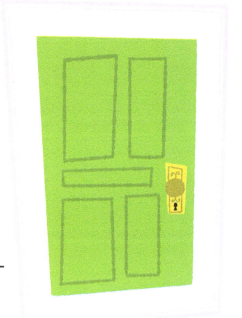

Write a sentence using one of these words.

_____

_____

Places, Please

Add each of your spelling words to this puzzle. Use the letters shown to help you. Write your word again in the blank.

roof _____   table _____

room _____   chairs _____

house _____   sink _____

door _____   stove _____

floor _____   broom _____

Finish the Poem

Finish this rhyming poem. Use one of the spelling words from the box in each blank. If time allows, draw a picture to go with your poem on another piece of paper.

room	door	house	table	broom	floor

I know a little mouse

Who has a little ___ ___ ___ ___ ___.

He opens a little ___ ___ ___ ___

And walks onto the ___ ___ ___ ___ ___.

He has a little ___ ___ ___ ___ ___

To sweep each little ___ ___ ___ ___.

And now if you are able,

Please help him set his ___ ___ ___ ___ ___!

Words to Learn: MORE AT HOME WORDS

Write each word in the blank.

1. carpet _____

2. lamp _____

3. sofa _____

4. couch _____

5. dishes _____

6. clock _____

7. window _____

8. bathtub _____

9. bedroom _____

10. mailbox _____

Write your hardest words again here:

_____

_____

_____

Word Search

Circle each word you find in the word search. Words may go up, down, across, or diagonally, both backward and forward. Write each word as you find it.

S	W	C	X	C	L	O	C	K	C
Q	R	I	V	O	H	I	V	A	A
P	I	Y	N	O	C	Y	M	C	V
B	D	W	M	D	U	T	O	A	V
M	A	I	L	B	O	X	O	R	A
W	P	T	S	U	C	W	R	P	F
U	M	U	H	H	B	B	D	E	O
B	A	O	R	T	E	B	E	T	S
S	L	U	L	T	U	S	B	D	N
I	L	B	N	U	A	B	N	U	M

window _____   lamp _____

clock _____   dishes _____

sofa _____   bathtub _____

couch _____   bedroom _____

carpet _____   mailbox _____

Be Choosy!

Choose the best answer and circle it. Write the word in the blank.

1. When I'm tired, I like to soak in the _____.

   carpet   bathtub   mailbox

2. My sister and I often help Dad do the _____.

   dishes   lamp   couch

3. We are going to be late. Look at the _____!

   clock   window   bedroom

4. Every day, I look in the _____, hoping to find
   something for me.

   lamp   mailbox   sofa

5. It is cold outside, so the _____ is foggy.

   couch   carpet   window

Tic-Tac-Toe

Circle every word that is spelled correctly. Draw a line through three correct words to score a tic-tac-toe. Write the misspelled words correctly on the lines below.

soffa	lamp	bedroom
dishs	carpet	mialbox
clock	bathub	cowch

_____

_____

_____

Letter Sense

Add the missing letters to your spelling words so each sentence makes sense.

1. Three of us can sit on the s ___ ___ ___ at one time.

2. At my house, we call this a c ___ ___ ___ ___.

3. Our floor looked old, but this new ___ ___ ___ p ___ t looks very nice!

4. I like to read in my b ___ ___ ___ ___ ___ m before I go to sleep.

5. Mom likes to read in the ___ ___ ___ h ___ ___ ___!

6. Our ___ l ___ ___ ___ makes a loud ticking sound.

Crack the Code

Use the code to find your spelling words. Write each letter as you solve it.

1. ‡ 8 4 5 » 4

   d — i — s — h — e — s

2. < £ 2 5 2 6 <

   b — a — t — h — t — u — b

3. 3 1 6 3 5

   c — o — u — c — h

4. ? 8 ✱ ‡ 1 ?

   w — i — n — d — o — w

5. 3 £ 7 ... » 2

   c — a — r — p — e — t

6. < » ‡ 7 1 1 ©

   b — e — d — r — o — o — m

1 = o	2 = t	3 = c
4 = s	5 = h	6 = u
7 = r	8 = i	» = e
✱ = n	... = p	‡ = d
< = b	£ = a	© = m
? = w		

Words to Learn: EVERYDAY WORDS

Write each word in the blank.

1. loud   _____

2. soft   _____

3. under   _____

4. over   _____

5. before   _____

6. after   _____

7. always   _____

8. never   _____

9. comes   _____

10. goes   _____

Write your hardest words again here:

_____

_____

_____

Match Up

When we write, some letters reach above the line and some go below it. Look at the shapes to help you find the right spelling word and write it in the matching shape.

under   after   goes   always   soft   before

1.
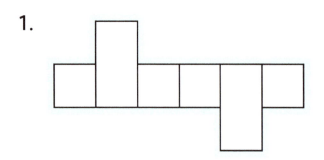

2.
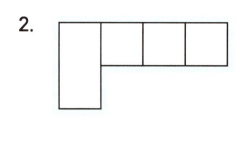

3.
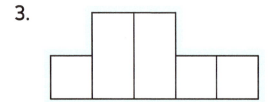

4.
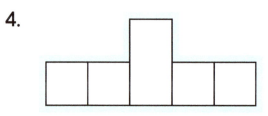

5.
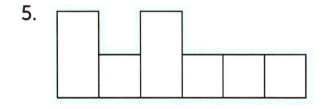

6.
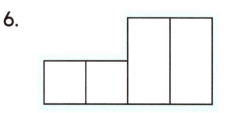

Line Up!

Draw a line from each word in List A to the word that means the opposite in List B. Write each word again in the line next to it.

List A

before _____

comes _____

loud _____

never _____

under _____

List B

soft _____

after _____

over _____

goes _____

always _____

Write a sentence using one of these words.

_____

_____

Merry-Go-Round

Start at any letter and move around the circle, either forward or backward, to find one of your spelling words. Circle the first letter. Write the word under each circle.

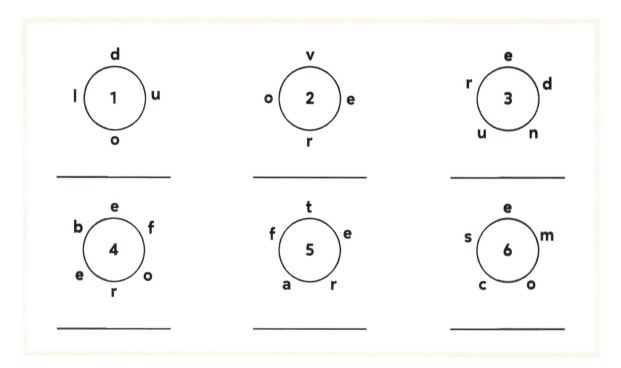

_____   _____   _____

_____   _____   _____

Box Stop

Write the correct word from the box in each blank. You will not use all the words.

always	under	comes	loud	before
never	over	goes	soft	after

1. My brother _____ to bed at nine o'clock.

2. I go to sleep _____ I read a story with my sister.

3. Sometimes our dog is so _____ that I wake up.

4. It is hard to train him to have a _____ bark!

5. I am happy in the morning. I am _____ glad to start

   a new day.

6. I don't like the day to end. I _____ want to go to bed!

Scrambles

Write the correct spelling word for each set of scrambled letters.

1. s o g e _____ _____ _____ _____

2. v e r e n _____ _____ _____ _____ _____

3. f r e e o b _____ _____ _____ _____ _____ _____

4. t r e f a _____ _____ _____ _____ _____

5. t s f o _____ _____ _____ _____

6. a l y a w s _____ _____ _____ _____ _____ _____

7. d n e u r _____ _____ _____ _____ _____

8. o d u l _____ _____ _____ _____

Write a sentence using one of these words.

_____

_____

Words to Learn: MORE EVERYDAY WORDS

Write each word in the blank.

1. very _____

2. every _____

3. sight _____

4. right _____

5. said _____

6. says _____

7. because _____

8. around _____

9. could _____

10. again _____

Write your hardest words again here:

_____

_____

_____

Be Choosy!

Choose the best answer and circle it. Write the word in the blank.

1. I go to the zoo _____ summer with my grandpa.

   very   every   right

2. It is a great day _____ my grandpa is a lot of fun.

   because   around   says

3. "Maybe we can go two times this year," he _____.

   said   sight   could

4. I hope we can go _____ soon!

   right   very   again

5. We will walk all the way _____ the zoo.

   around   because   right

6. Then we will have a snack and do it _____!

   sight   every   again

Tic-Tac-Toe

Circle every word that is spelled correctly. Draw a line through three correct words to score a tic-tac-toe. Write the misspelled words correctly in the blanks.

becuase	around	cuold
agian	says	right
sigt	very	siad

_____

_____

_____

Follow the Clues

Write the spelling words that fit each clue. There will be several answers at first. You will write some spelling words more than once. For the last clue, there will be just one word. Which word will it be?

again	around	because	could	very
every	sight	right	said	says

1. Five words spelled with five letters

    _____ _____ _____

    _____ _____

2. Two words spelled with five letters and that rhyme with each other

    _____ _____

3. One word, spelled with five letters, that rhymes with another word on the list and is the opposite of left

    _____

Word Search

Circle each word you find in the word search. Words may go up, down, across, or diagonally, both backward and forward. Write each word as you find it.

B	B	R	I	G	H	T	D
A	J	E	D	F	H	H	Y
V	R	C	C	N	A	G	R
E	S	O	S	A	B	I	E
R	A	U	U	A	U	S	V
Y	I	L	Z	N	Y	S	E
U	D	D	R	W	D	S	E
N	I	A	G	A	W	X	Z

because _____   sight _____

again _____   said _____

around _____   says _____

could _____   every _____

right _____   very _____

Finish the Poem

Finish this rhyming poem. Use one of the spelling words from the box in each blank. If time allows, draw a picture to go with your poem on another piece of paper.

around	Could	again	said	sight	right

Our brown cat was white!

What a __ __ __ __ __!

Is she all __ __ __ __ __?

We looked all __ __ __ __ __ __

Until we found

A pail of white paint!

__ __ __ __ __ we wash our cat?

Would she go along with that?

We tried again and __ __ __ __ __ and yet . . .

Dad __ __ __ __ we should call the vet!

PUZZLE 91

Letter Sense: Double Consonants

Add the correct set of double letters to your spelling words so each sentence makes sense.

1. The clown's hat was very fu ___ ___ y.

2. The orange bu___ ___ erfly is so pretty!

3. The clown gave a boy a ba ___ ___ oon.

4. The boy was very ha ___ ___ y!

5. Have you ever petted a ra___ ___ it ?

6. Have you held a new ki ___ ___ en?

7. I am glad we are in the same cla ___ ___ .

8. We can help each other learn to spe ___ ___ new words.

9. Do you know how to a ___ ___ big numbers?

10. My dad's bu ___ ___ y likes to come to our house.

11. He helps my dad cut the gra ___ ___ .

12. He never gets cro ___ ___ with me.

13. My dad looks si ___ ___ y when he wears his big red nose.

14. Sometimes he wears big ye ___ ___ ow ears, too!

Places, Please: Long Vowel Sounds

You learned many words with long vowel sounds. Some of these words follow the vowel-consonant-silent e pattern, as in *side* and *lake*.

Finish spelling each word you learned by adding the missing vowel and the silent e at the end. Then place each finished word into the puzzle. (The letters already in the puzzle may help you.)

j __ k __   f __ v __

s __ f __   g r __ d __

w h __ l __   s t __ v __

s n __ k __   s l __ d __

w h __ t __   n __ n __

PUZZLE 93

PUZZLE 93

Scrambles: Short and Long Vowels

Unscramble these words that have just one vowel. Write S in the box after the word if the vowel has a short sound (as in *cat*). Write L in the box after the word if the vowel has a long sound (as in *most*).

1. d s a ___ ___ ___ ☐
2. h t a p ___ ___ ___ ___ ☐
3. t o f s ___ ___ ___ ___ ☐
4. l i c d h ___ ___ ___ ___ ___ ☐
5. o g d ___ ___ ___ ☐
6. s f i h ___ ___ ___ ___ ☐
7. k n i s ___ ___ ___ ___ ☐
8. m l a p ___ ___ ___ ___ ☐
9. x i s ___ ___ ___ ☐
10. n p o d ___ ___ ___ ___ ☐
11. l g d o ___ ___ ___ ___ ☐
12. u p j m ___ ___ ___ ___ ☐
13. c u k d ___ ___ ___ ___ ☐
14. e k s d ___ ___ ___ ___ ☐

Write a sentence that uses one of the S words.

_____

_____

Write a sentence that uses one of the L words.

_____

_____

PUZZLE 94

Be Choosy! Consonant Blends

Many spelling words begin with consonant blends. Choose the best consonant blend for each sentence. Circle the blend and write the whole word in the blank.

1. There are so many ___ ___ees in the park. _____

   sh   tr   fr

2. A ___ ___ail carries a shell on its back. _____

   sn   ch   sh

3. I want to learn to ___ ___ip. _____

   gr   tr   sk

4. Let's ___ ___udy our math facts. _____

   st   cl   sh

5. My ___ ___andma made this shirt for me. _____

   br   gr   fr

6. When the lights went out, the room was ___ ___ack. _____

   gr   st   bl

7. My ___ ___other was happy on his birthday. _____

   cl   br   tr

8. I know how to ___ ___aw a duck. _____

   sh   pr   dr

9. I am very ___ ___oud of my little sister. _____

   pr   fl   ch

10. Will you be my ___ ___iend? _____

   br   bl   fr

Super Tic-Tac-Toe: Vowel Teams

Some spelling words have tricky vowel teams. Circle all the words that are spelled correctly on this big tic-tac-toe game. Then draw a line to connect FOUR correct words in a row. Write the other words correctly in the lines below.

blue	gruop	learn	aroond
cuoch	eihgt	four	house
gaot	luagh	air	taem
because	agian	mean	read

_____

_____

_____

_____

PUZZLE 96

Merry-Go-Rounds: Two-Syllable Words

You learned many words with two syllables. Can you find 12 of them on these merry-go-rounds? Start at any letter and move around the circle, either forward or backward, to find one of your spelling words. Circle the first letter. Write the word under each circle.

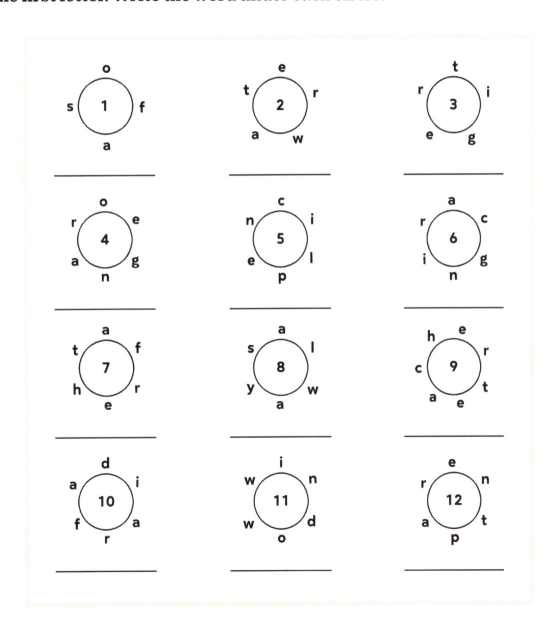

Hidden Message: Word Endings

For each clue, choose a word from the box plus a word ending. Write the complete word in the white squares in the puzzle. You will spell an answer to the riddle:

What should you do when you find an elephant asleep in your bed?

Words:

chair	pet
gloom	tree
joy	flower
bore	help
toy	camp
game	thank
kite	scare
hope	bird
dish	

Endings:

-s or –es

-ing

-ful

-y

-ed or –d

1. Animal friends
2. Feeling down or blue
3. Full of fear
4. Large plants with trunks
5. Staying outside in tents
6. Places to sit
7. Full of joy
8. Things you can play
9. Fly these in the sky with string on a windy day
10. Blooms
11. Full of thanks
12. How you feel when there is nothing to do
13. Animals that fly
14. Full of hope
15. Plates, cups, and bowls
16. Gives help
17. Blocks, cars, dolls, games, and more

1												
2												
3												
4												
5												
6												
7												
8												
9												
10												
11												
12												
13												
14												
15												
16												
17												
						e						

What should you do when you find an elephant asleep in your bed?

___ ___ ___ ___ ___ ___   ___ ___ ___ ___ ___ ___ ___ ___ ___   ___ ___ ___e!

ANSWER KEY

PUZZLE 1

1. baby
2. aunt
3. sister
4. family
5. uncle
6. brother

PUZZLE 2

uncle, aunt
mother, brother,
   father, sister
baby, family, home, pets

PUZZLE 3

1. father
2. mother
3. uncle
4. aunt
5. sister
6. brother
7. home
8. pets

PUZZLE 4

PUZZLE 5

1. uncle
2. baby
3. father
4. pets
5. sister

PUZZLE 6

Corrections: grandpa,
caring, together, sharing

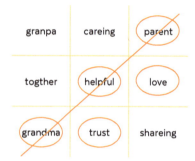

PUZZLE 7

PUZZLE 8

1. together
2. parent
3. grandma
4. love
5. sharing

PUZZLE 9

1. trust
2. sharing
3. love
4. grandpa
5. parent
6. grandma

PUZZLE 10

1. home
2. trust
3. sharing
4. child
5. parent
6. caring
7. helpful
8. together

PUZZLE 11

1. grin
2. group
3. toys
4. funny
5. games
6. outside
7. buddy
8. inside

PUZZLE 12

1. pal, buddy
2. group, team
3. inside, outside
4. toys, games

PUZZLE 13

T	F	E	D	I	S	T	U	O
H	S	Z	F	S	Y	O	T	A
L	G	I	N	S	I	D	E	E
E	R	G	U	Y	N	N	U	F
S	O	R	E	Q	L	M	V	T
P	U	I	A	J	K	N	R	E
A	P	N	W	Y	V	R	L	A
L	W	G	A	M	E	S	N	M
X	Y	Y	D	D	U	B	M	I

PUZZLE 14

Corrections: buddy, toys, group, funny, outside

PUZZLE 15

PUZZLE 16

1. laugh
2. give
3. talk
4. listen
5. party
6. joke

PUZZLE 17

1. talk
2. joke
3. friend
4. party
5. laugh
6. listen
7. children
8. balloon

PUZZLE 18

1. birthday
2. children
3. joke
4. give
5. balloon

PUZZLE 19

1. balloon
2. friend
3. birthday
4. listen
5. children
6. laugh

PUZZLE 20

1. friend
2. laugh, joke
3. listen
4. party, birthday
5. talk

PUZZLE 21

1. learn
2. think
3. paint
4. spell
5. count
6. write

PUZZLE 22

spell, learn, read
work, write, draw, add
paint, think, count

PUZZLE 23

Corrections: spell, learn, count, draw, work

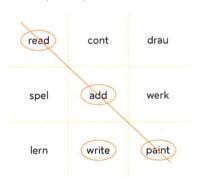

PUZZLE 24

1. read
2. learn
3. count
4. add
5. work

PUZZLE 25

PUZZLE 26

1. pencil
2. teacher
3. shelf
4. study
5. paper
6. desk
7. backpack
8. lunchroom

PUZZLE 27

1. grade
2. class
3. shelf
4. teacher
5. pencil
6. study

PUZZLE 28

1. class or grade
2. shelf, desk, backpack
3. teacher
4. lunchroom
5. study
6. pencil

PUZZLE 29

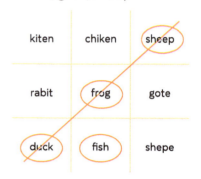

PUZZLE 30

1. pencil
2. shelf
3. grade
4. desk
5. teacher
6. paper
7. backpack
8. class

PUZZLE 31

dog, frog, goat
rabbit, kitten, chicken, duck
fish, sheep, horse

PUZZLE 32

1. horse
2. sheep
3. kitten
4. frog
5. rabbit
6. duck

PUZZLE 33

1. chicken
2. dog
3. sheep
4. kitten
5. duck

PUZZLE 34

Corrections: kitten, chicken, rabbit, goat, sheep

kiten	chiken	sheep
rabit	frog	gote
duck	fish	shepe

PUZZLE 35

1. dog, kitten, rabbit, sheep, goat, horse
2. kitten, rabbit
3. rabbit

PUZZLE 36

1. camel
2. tiger
3. goose
4. snake
5. ladybug
6. whale
7. shark
8. butterfly

PUZZLE 37

1. whale, snail
2. snail, snake
3. goose, ladybug, butterfly
4. whale, shark
5. Answers will vary.

PUZZLE 38

1. whale
2. camel
3. lion
4. goose
5. tiger
6. snake

PUZZLE 39

L	C	E	L	E	N	O	I	L
I	G	L	E	S	H	A	R	K
A	E	A	M	O	V	K	Y	D
N	E	H	A	O	E	V	G	B
S	L	W	C	G	T	H	P	V
Y	L	F	R	E	T	T	U	B
T	I	G	E	R	H	U	T	R
U	C	L	A	D	Y	B	U	G
J	P	Q	G	E	K	A	N	S

PUZZLE 40

1. snail
2. goose
3. whale
4. snake
5. tiger
6. shark

PUZZLE 41

walk, water, trees, grass, air
climb, jump, skip
pond, pool

PUZZLE 42

1. water
2. climb
3. pool
4. walk
5. skip

PUZZLE 43

1. walk, jump,
   skip, climb
2. Answers will vary.
3. pond, pool
4. trees, grass
5. Answers will vary.

PUZZLE 44

1. walk
2. grass
3. jump
4. water
5. pool
6. pond
7. climb
8. skip

PUZZLE 45

1. air
2. trees
3. jump
4. pond
5. grass
6. Water

PUZZLE 46

1. kites
2. slide
3. camping
4. sandbox
5. sunshine
6. flowers

PUZZLE 47

P	C	G	R	K	I	T	E	S	C	D
U	L	G	N	I	P	M	A	C	K	X
B	D	A	X	R	J	F	L	Z	O	X
B	I	M	Y	I	Q	I	B	B	G	F
F	X	R	S	G	O	B	D	Y	H	L
U	M	R	D	B	R	N	T	S	T	O
D	N	I	W	S	A	O	E	Q	A	W
Z	H	L	K	S	W	D	U	Q	P	E
S	U	N	S	H	I	N	E	N	R	R
L	R	L	Y	L	V	W	B	T	D	S
A	N	G	S	W	E	G	A	I	H	O

PUZZLE 48

1. playground
2. wind
3. path
4. sandbox
5. flowers

PUZZLE 49

1. birds
2. wind
3. slide
4. flowers
5. kites
6. sandbox

PUZZLE 50

1. kites, flowers, birds
2. kites, birds
3. birds

PUZZLE 51

1. red
2. yellow
3. gold
4. blue
5. purple
6. white
7. orange
8. black

PUZZLE 52

1. gold
2. black
3. yellow, orange
4. white
5. blue
6. brown
7. purple

PUZZLE 53

Corrections: red, yellow, blue, purple, brown

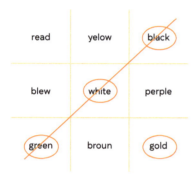

PUZZLE 54

1. blue
2. green
3. gold
4. brown
5. orange
6. purple
7. yellow
8. white

PUZZLE 55

PUZZLE 56

1. four
2. seven
3. eight
4. eleven
5. zero
6. seven

PUZZLE 57

B	V	X	P	N	E	V	E	S
O	E	F	I	E	V	X	I	S
R	S	L	W	U	I	F	W	E
E	K	T	E	D	N	G	X	S
Z	O	M	W	V	Y	I	H	O
E	F	Z	J	E	E	J	N	T
R	M	O	A	M	L	N	L	E
N	E	T	U	F	I	V	E	S
Q	N	A	R	R	L	Z	E	T

PUZZLE 58

four, zero
nine, ten, seven, eleven
six, five, eight, twelve

PUZZLE 59

1. five, seven, nine, eleven
2. seven, eleven
3. eleven

PUZZLE 60

0	zero
1	one
2	two
3	three
4	four
5	five
6	six
7	seven
8	eight
9	nine
10	ten
11	eleven
12	twelve
13	thirteen
14	fourteen

PUZZLE 61

1. glad
2. silly
3. scared
4. lost
5. strong
6. angry

PUZZLE 62

1. glad, sad
2. glad
3. angry
4. silly
5. scared
6. Answers will vary.

PUZZLE 63

1. safe
2. silly
3. scared
4. lost
5. strong
6. angry

PUZZLE 64

1. happy
2. lost
3. glad
4. angry
5. silly
6. sad
7. scared
8. strong

PUZZLE 65

PUZZLE 66

gloomy, joyful,
   hopeful, thankful
sorry, cross, bored
hurt, proud, afraid

PUZZLE 67

1. proud
2. bored
3. hopeful
4. afraid
5. cross
6. thankful

PUZZLE 68

Corrections: bored, afraid,
gloomy, hurt, hopeful

PUZZLE 69

PUZZLE 70

1. joyful
2. sorry, hurt
3. gloomy
4. bored
5. hopeful
6. proud

PUZZLE 71

1. room, broom
2. house
3. floor, door
4. sink
5. roof
6. Answers will vary.

PUZZLE 72

1. roof
2. sink
3. floor
4. chairs
5. house
6. stove

PUZZLE 73

1. floor
2. broom
3. sink
4. stove
5. door
6. house
7. chairs
8. table

PUZZLE 74

(crossword grid with words: CHAIRS, DOOR, SINK, HOUSE, STOVE, TABLE, FLOOR, BROOM, ROOM)

PUZZLE 75

house, door, floor, broom,
room, table

PUZZLE 76

```
S W C X C L O C K C
Q R I V O H I V A A
P I Y N O C Y M C V
B D W M D U T O A V
M A I L B O X O R A
W P T S U C W R P F
U M U H H B B D E O
B A O R T E B E T S
S L U L T U S B D N
I L B N U A B N U M
```

PUZZLE 77

1. bathtub
2. dishes
3. clock
4. mailbox
5. window

PUZZLE 78

Corrections: sofa, dishes, mailbox, bathtub, couch

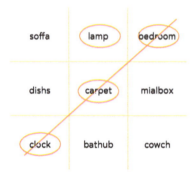

PUZZLE 79

1. sofa
2. couch
3. carpet
4. bedroom
5. bathtub
6. clock

PUZZLE 80

1. dishes
2. bathtub
3. couch
4. window
5. carpet
6. bedroom

PUZZLE 81

1. always
2. goes
3. after
4. under
5. before
6. soft

PUZZLE 82

before-after
comes-goes
loud-soft
never-always
under-over

PUZZLE 83

1. loud
2. over
3. under
4. before
5. after
6. comes

PUZZLE 84

1. goes
2. after
3. loud
4. soft
5. always
6. never

PUZZLE 85

1. goes
2. never
3. before
4. after
5. soft
6. always
7. under
8. loud

PUZZLE 86

1. every
2. because
3. said
4. again
5. around
6. again

PUZZLE 87

Corrections: because, could, again, sight, said

PUZZLE 88

1. again, could, every, sight, right
2. sight, right
3. right

PUZZLE 89

B	B	R	I	G	H	T	D
A	J	E	D	F	H	H	Y
V	R	C	C	N	A	G	R
E	S	O	S	A	B	I	E
R	A	U	U	A	U	S	V
Y	I	L	Z	N	Y	S	E
U	D	D	R	W	D	S	E
N	I	A	G	A	W	X	Z

PUZZLE 90

sight, right, around, Could, again, said

PUZZLE 91

1. funny
2. butterfly
3. balloon
4. happy
5. rabbit
6. kitten
7. class
8. spell
9. add
10. buddy
11. grass
12. cross
13. silly
14. yellow

PUZZLE 92

1. joke
2. safe
3. whale
4. snake
5. white
6. five
7. grade
8. stove
9. slide
10. nine

PUZZLE 93

(Some have more than one possible answer. This book's spelling words are shown here.)

1. sad   S
2. path   S
3. soft   S
4. child   L
5. dog   S
6. fish   S
7. sink   S
8. lamp   S
9. six   S
10. pond   S
11. gold   L
12. jump   S
13. duck   S
14. desk   S

Answers will vary.

PUZZLE 94

1. tr, trees
2. sn, snail
3. sk, skip
4. st, study
5. gr, grandma
6. bl, black
7. br, brother
8. dr, draw
9. pr, proud
10. fr, friend

PUZZLE 95

Corrections: group, around, couch, eight, goat, laugh, team, again

blue	gruop	learn	aroond
cuoch	eihgt	four	house
gaot	luagh	air	taem
because	agian	mean	read

PUZZLE 96

1. sofa
2. water
3. tiger
4. orange
5. pencil
6. caring
7. father
8. always
9. teacher
10. afraid
11. window
12. parent

PUZZLE 97

#												
1			p	e	t	s						
2				g	l	o	o	m	y			
3		s	c	a	r	e	d					
4			t	r	e	e	s					
5			c	a	m	p	i	n	g			
6	c	h	a	i	r	s						
7					j	o	y	f	u	l		
8				g	a	m	e	s				
9			k	i	t	e	s					
10			f	l	o	w	e	r	s			
11					t	h	a	n	k	f	u	l
12			b	o	r	e	d					
13				b	i	r	d	s				
14			h	o	p	e	f	u	l			
15		d	i	s	h	e	s					
16				h	e	l	p	f	u	l		
17			t	o	y	s						
						e						

SLEEP SOMEWHERE ELSE!

ACKNOWLEDGMENTS

I would like to thank:

EclipseCrossword puzzle engine ©Green Eclipse, available for free use at EclipseCrossword.com.

Word Search Creator V1.0 © Matthew Wellings.

Dictionaries that gave me ideas for some of my puzzles—in particular, two longtime favorites from my personal bookshelf:

Abate, Frank, ed. *Oxford Desktop Dictionary and Thesaurus, American Edition*. New York: Berkley Books, 1997.

de Mello Vianna, Fernando, ed. *Children's Dictionary*. Boston: Houghton Mifflin, 1979.

My husband, Keith, who was always ready to wash dishes, fold laundry, and run errands to allow me more time to write. He's the best!

ABOUT THE AUTHOR

Ann Richmond Fisher is a former classroom teacher. She's also a wife and mother. She's known these days as "Granny Annie" to two beloved children whose middle names just happen to be Jane and Karl!

Ann has a degree in elementary education from Northern Michigan University. After teaching in a classroom for six years, Ann chose to be a stay-at-home mom to her two children, Bryce and Betsy. Her love for teaching, learning, and words drew her to the world of freelance writing. She sold her first puzzles to *Highlights for Children* when her kids were preschoolers.

She's published more than 60 books, posters, and other products for a dozen publishers. She owns two websites: Spelling-Words-Well.com and Word-Game-World.com.

Printed in the USA
CPSIA information can be obtained
at www.ICGtesting.com
JSHW072353210624
65006JS00005B/8